from
LIFE to LIFE

a collection of poetry and prose

ELTON BULLER

From the Life to Life: A Collection of Poetry and Prose

Copyright © 2020 Elton Buller. All rights reserved. No part of this book may be reproduced or retransmitted in any form or by any means without the written permission of the publisher.

Published by Wheatmark®
2030 East Speedway Boulevard, Suite 106
Tucson, Arizona 85719 USA
www.wheatmark.com

ISBN: 978-1-62787-757-2 (paperback)
ISBN: 978-1-62787-758-9 (ebook)
LCCN: 2019915139

Bulk-ordering discounts are available through Wheatmark, Inc. For more information, e-mail orders@wheatmark.com or call 1-888-934-0888.

rev202001

Contents

Acknowledgments

Thanks to Stan and Connie Benjamin for inspiring me to have this book published for all to read.

Thanks to Susan P. for giving me the inspiration to put onto paper how I felt in the beginning of my journey.

I also recognize J. Peterson for the poems on pages 1, 2, and 5: for giving me the courage to write on my own without assistance.

Most of all, thanks to Kathryn Sayre for inspiration to publish my writings, typing, editing and making sure my writings got to the publisher and making my journey complete.

About the Author

This section tells a little about the author, Elton Neil Buller.

Throughout Pomeroy High School, I was a tremendous athlete, earning A-Team letters from freshman to senior years in sports. Upon graduation, I was accepted by and attended Eastern Washington State University until a calamity happened.

I had come back to Pomeroy two weeks before completing my first year of college in 1968, when I was involved in a major auto accident. My best friend was killed, and the EMT's thought I was dead. Barely alive, I was rushed to Spokane, Washington, where I lay in a deep coma for one month. After I showed signs of waking from the coma, my lead doctor, Dr. R. J. Weiland, transferred me down to Pomeroy Health Care Center, where I fell in and out of comatose status for the next several months. Upon regaining consciousness, I had lost the ability to walk and talk. After several months of therapy, these attributes slowly came back to me. It has taken me many years to recover almost to 100 percent from the injuries inflicted upon me.

In 1971, I earned my forestry/conservation degree and rejoined the workforce for the US Forestry Services. Upon leaving the US Forestry, I went to work for the Washington State Patrol. However, my extensive injuries would permit me to stay there only one year.

While employed by the US Forestry Department in 1967, I started writing poetry and prose. After the auto accident, I was not able to write. I took it up again as I started on my journey of healing.

In the contents of this book, you can somewhat tell my stages of recovery and development. Going from being near "vegetable" status to what I am today is something of a miracle. Thank you, Lord!

Death
August 1967

I have no friends to claim me
But I have many enemies to maim me
I must be ready to die alone
For each man must reap what he has sown
Dying really wouldn't be so bad
When you look back on the life you had.

Do not fear sweet death
For only it can set you free
Welcome that joyous last breath
That will deliver you from life's drudgery
Whether you were happy or blue
The choice was made by you.

Be it right or wrong,
We can now sing our song.

In the Valley of the Shadow
August 1967

As I look back on my young loves
Although at the time they seemed to be true
I realize I was foolish in mind and heart
And after every one I told myself I was through.
I used to lie awake at nights in contemplation
And at the same time gaze into an unending space
Where the mighty bodies lie in anticipation
As to where their heavenly masses would end the race
And wish I were they with no soul and heart
Only to be their own rulers in such a lifeless place
But then I would be dead and not have a start
In an ever-eventful, unpeaceful world without a heart.

The uncontrollable power swept over me early in life
And caused me to gaze at the opposite sex
Not knowing that before too long one would be my wife
Having over me the power of an Olympic god's hex.
Most young boys choose without giving much hesitation
But for me I choose with patience and care
Because I know once I choose, I yield everything to her
And know it I do my heart would tear
If I don't pick the girl with the right hair.

With each girl I chose I left a part of me
Until now I know not when to love
Or if or if not my heart belongs to the sea
For it is as undecided as a newborn dove,
In time after time leave me they did
Not to realize the hardship and pain they left behind
But to turn to another and to me farewell they bid
Thinking I would forget and my heart would unwind.
And forget not did I the many lies they impeached
Upon me as nothing I believed they ever said before

But now I realize I am thinking and crying
Of the girl who makes me wish I was dying.

As I sit here with tears filling my eyes
While the storm rages through the night
The clouds blot out the stars in the skies
Leaving me alone in darkness, praying for light.
She said that for her I was the only one
But still she held this fear deep in her heart
That possibly I was not the only light of the sun.
To me on this dreadful night this truth did impart
Prior to this time she had given her heart to me
Now she says she thinks there could be another.

I sit here looking upon the forever-rolling sea
Watching the lonely waves crashing upon each other
Thundering upon the rocks at every hand
Sending their mighty spumes high into the air
While churning the once-mighty monoliths to sand
Just as her wicked lies my heart did tear
Till no longer can it laugh or sing.

Now I must walk in the Valley of the Shadow
Traveling alone, constantly seeking
The happiness my heart will not know.
I hope someday soon I will escape this fate
And will find something to call mine
And the joyous freedom this does create
Then will finally make the sun forever shine.

Believe in them I did,
Till no longer can I stand
Knowing that they
Will always hold the upper hand.

She

September 1967

I think of her often
She thinks not of me.

I talk of her often
She talks not of me.

I think of my love for her
She thinks naught of me.

I live not without her
She lives without me.

I am me
She is she.

Sorrow

August 1967

It is locked in the breast
Though we may want to shed tears
It is more often the best
To carry it through the long years.

For then it will be truly felt
And prevent us from again,
Because its icy stab will not melt,
Causing the injured one the same pain.

It is better not to be spoken
As we can most clearly see
Because its sincerity would be broken
And we only speak a mockery.

Because very seldom can we say what we feel
We can't always express it as we should
So it is best our lips we seal
Before it does more harm than good.

The sounds that silence makes
In the direction the path takes.

Her

1968 and 1969

The sound, smell, and sight of a babbling brook rushing through a meadow so green. Birds singing their evening lullaby as the sun slowly sinks beyond the yonder mountain. The rising moon takes its places high in the heavens to guard the Earth against intruders.

But a girl of softness, sweetness, and tenderness sits upon my mind. She holds beauty deep within her breast, she holds kindness deep within her heart, and she holds wisdom deep within her mind.

I touch her with my mind, but she is unreal to my fingertips. She is like a storm tearing at the sea, building wave upon wave only to send them crashing and pounding to a calm but mighty shore.

Every throb of my heart reflects the image of her, every thought I have is filled with her wholeness, only for her to be sitting there with her precious little hands folded in her tiny, delicate lap. Her big, brown, golden eyes searching the area for that something that I wish she would find in me.

Only to lie here with her fantasy tearing at my heart leaves me in much sadness as tears trickle down my cheek.

Chances
1969

The tide rolls in, the trees wave gently with the wind. The clouds float by, and I walk on. I stroll on reaching high into the sky, never to find what I am reaching for. It seems an endless game.

Whatever the game is, I will play it because I take chances throughout my life. The chances I take sometimes endanger my life. Yet anything we do we take a chance on our very existence.

We could be walking through a forest when a tree crashes down upon us or taking a hike when a rock tears loose and down the hill it rolls to hit us, or any of the other chances we take daily in life.

Life in general is a chance.

I Would Like
1969

I would like to walk in your gentle footsteps, or sit upon your shoe to execute each move you make with your own little touch of precision. It would be like walking in Heaven to gently glide along with the gentle rhythmic motion of a pendulum.

Or I would like to sit upon every volume of breath emitted from your soft, pleasant throat, as the calmness of a gentle breeze blowing on an ice-cold mountain lake on a calm, cool summer night.

I would like to sit upon your brain for the most precious instant to contemplate the thought of me as you slowly perceive me as I come within your vision. It would be like sitting upon a cirrus cloud gently floating through the span of atmosphere, never to know containment.

Mostly, I would like to sit upon your warm and sympathetic heart and experience each tear you shed with agony, sympathy, and love—it would be such ecstasy.

Standing near you is like sitting near a beach fire, the warmth radiated from your body is like no other comparable source.

To live within your life for the most delicate second would be like enforcing a dream into reality.

To experience these thoughts is like the constant beating a coastline takes through the relentless, never-ending torment taken from its enemy the sea, slowly tearing you apart pebble by pebble.

Mother Earth
1969

The mountains glitter in the background, the sun fades into
shadows, the different grasses quietly lie down, and the bull elk
majestically looks around.

He doesn't see much, only the smaller bulls and cows he leads
throughout the tree-stricken land.

Here I sit, all alone with no one near. But I am not alone!
Because there are the grasses, the trees, the flowers, and the
rippling waters to comfort me, and Mother Earth.

The bull gently turns his head from left to right, observing
every movement that transpires within his circle. He sees the
mountains slowly fade from sight into the West as light slowly
diminishes.

A soft breeze is blowing, bringing the scent of pine trees strong
into the nostrils as they sing their evening lullaby, as darkness
slowly creeps upon us.

The bull squats down until he rests cheek to cheek against
Mother Earth, bidding good evening to all those in his herd.
Also as if to say through his untold words,

"I love you, Mother Earth, and your many children!"

My Heart

1969

Once again I walk the streets alone
On the outside I am unchanged
On the inside my heart is weak
I ask, "Is it always me?"
No one can answer it better than the person within
He tells me I am foolish.
He tells me my heart is a flower
When a light comes along it opens up
When the light is extracted it withers away.
On the outside I am unchanged
On the inside my heart is weak.

Problems

1969

As I sit here in contemplation, the world spins on and on, not caring what happens to me. If it did, it would be so confused as to stop spinning!

My problems are but nothing to those of others, but to me, they mean something very special.

I would sometimes like to sit upon my brain and observe what it thinks and *if* it thinks! Every thought would be a new experience, and after these experiences, I would like to stop and recall all that took place during them.

Problems, problems, what would life be like without them? My life is full of them, just like everyone else's life. I guess you could say life wouldn't be life without problems.

What is life?

Life is too complex for we humans to understand. No one has the power or right to try to define life, other than the maker of life itself.

My life is full of problems, as I said before. I can never be sure of anything without the fear of problems arising.

But, then, my outlook upon life is turning dire. If I could choose between life and death, I would choose to die. Dying would be a relief in this problem-filled world, a relief thought about quite often by me.

For, you see, my problems throw a heavy burden upon me at this moment. A burden so heavy as to slow me down on life's never-ending journey.

A never-ending journey to nowhere! A journey that goes on through the mist and further, whether problems arise or they don't.

You see, my reader, I have got problems! Some people have them, others think they don't, but everyone I say, everyone knows what I am talking about.

The Elements

1969

They call me the wind
They call me the rain
Together as one
But never the same.

I blow from the East
I blow from the West
Never from the same directions
Always at my best.

I rustle the grass
I rustle the tree
I am very alone
And still very free.

Life depends upon me
Without me, it would die
For nature depends upon me
Though seeing me brings a sigh.

They call me the wind
They call me the rain
Together as one
But never the same.

To Burn

1969

Your picture is planted deep within my heart,
And I hope you come back to me someday.
My love for you will never depart
Whatever you do or whatever you say.

Always it is like this
Whichever way it seems I turn.
I am a catalyst
Into a reactor I'm injected to burn.

Be Born

1970

A portion of the world dies with each heartbeat yet is to be born
again between each heartbeat.

The order of life is to be born, live, die, and be born again.

Who is to judge which phase of life is the most prominent?

I think death is the most significant phase of existence because if
you live a worthy life, you can die worthy.

Live your life exquisitely, proliferately, and to its fullest because
you will never get another chance in its human form.

Life—to be born, live, die, and be born again.

Live a worthy life and die worthy.

In the Hollow of His Hand
1970

In the hollow of His hand I lie
And in the hollow of His hand I will die.

Like nothing before I will ever envy
Or like anything I will ever see.

In the hollow of His hand we all enjoy
The happiness of a girl or boy.

Yes, in the hollow of His hand
Is swaying with He going across the land.

In the hollow of His hand we do believe
While others try to deceive.

In the hollow of His hand we accept a new face
And watch all the people race.

In the hollow of His hand we lie
And in the hollow of His hand we all die.

Open Doorway
1970

A light shines from an open doorway, the summer night makes
not a sound. Only the pine trees can be heard smothering the
Earth with the soft rustling of good-night.

I sit with not a friend on Earth, except for God. Only He guides
my path. He tells me not to worry, fret, or cry, but still I do. He
tells me to trust in Him, and all will be well. Romans 8:28 (All
things happen for the better to those who believe in God).

Once again I see the light peering from the open doorway, once
again I hear the pine trees, once again I realize that only God is
my companion.

The light has a luring power, not letting me turn away. The light
grows stronger, as do I. The light grows dimmer, as do I. The
light has more power than do I, as it can appear and diminish at
any time, whereas I cannot appear and reappear as I desire.

The light constantly illuminating from the open doorway,
like an eternal flame burning constantly, never ending, never
ceasing, and always there. As it is:
From an open doorway.

Perfect

1970

Eyes like two perfect crystals set side by side, simultaneously
rotating like scanning technical eyes conceiving everything
observed.

A gentle voice like the most perfect note ever exemplified by an
instrument ever produced.

Brunette hair like the most perfect hazel sunray to ever beat
down upon the Earth with the gentlest touch of a raindrop
falling down from a sky of gray.

And a heart as warm as the heat emitted from a cool, clear
night's beach fire, radiating warmth to all who receive it.
Perfect!

The Wind
1970

The reason blows with the wind
Softly today, furiously tomorrow.
Blowing everywhere
But never the same.

I wish I had the power of the wind
Calm at times while violent at others.
Blowing the sea waves gently
While tearing at the skies.

The wind that blew the trees of yesterday
Creating a mighty blast
Blows the trees of today
While blowing the blades of grass.

It tears particles from Mother Earth
Only to build a new mountain.
It kisses a newborn tree
And blows spray from the fountain.

The wind blows the trees of tomorrow
And kisses the grains of sands.
The wind cools a heart of sorrow
And tears a pole from where it stands.

The reason is never the same
The wind never blows the same.
The sea is never the same
But I love the wind most of all.

It is life for the birds of May
It tears pinecones from trees.
It makes flowers of today sway
But I do love the wind most of all.

Grain of Sand

1971

I am a grain of sand
Often blown many a mile.
Passed from hand to hand
Or to lie there all the while.

Whatever the case
I seem to never change.
Always ending up in the same place
Makes me feel like a boomerang.

Many times I'm found sitting upon a knee
Or sitting upon the beach.
At others, I'm found in the sea
But usually ending up back on the beach.

Sometimes blown many yards
Or picked up by a fish.
Often ending up on the boulevard
Or in the middle of a goldfish.

I am a grain of sand
Most often doing a dance across the sea or land
Never having time for romance.

Whatever the case may be
I seem to never change my name.
Even when I am blown against a tree
I am always a grain of sand.

In the Sky
1971

I see many things from the space I occupy
I see them on the land, and I see them in the sky.
I see them laugh, I see them dance
Sometimes I see them make romance.
I am a tree that stands so tall and high
Humans gaze at me from where they lie.
They have picnics all around
And here I stand, not making a sound.
They travel around here and there
They leave a mess I cannot bare.

Once I wish they would let me be
For then I would grow straight and very free.
Instead they cut off all my pitch
Because they know it makes a fire very rich.
Here it is I'm whittled away
At evening and through the day.
They don't stop at one piece or possibly two
They try to whittle me all the way through.
When they whittle me all the way through
I will kiss lip to lip with the morning dew
Because, you see, I will die
And no longer stand high in the sky.

That I Love

1971

I hear the soft breathing of the girl that I love, walking beside
me, as we walk in the rain as it gently falls from a sky of gray.

She hardly ever utters a word from her delicate little throat
about what she feels for and of me. She doesn't have to because
she tells me with every precious move she executes with her
own little touch of precision.

As she walks, she holds her chin high with dignity, with the
ability to make others look at her and envy her. She has the
appeal that makes men stop whatever they are doing and gaze at
her.

The girl that I love is special. There isn't another girl like her
around anywhere. She has the beauty to hold my eye, she has
the kindness to hold my heart, she is the ease within a sigh, she
is the happiness in my heart. She is the girl that I love, and I do
love her!

The Illusion

1971

She slowly, very passionately put her arms around me as she
pressed her warm, fragile lips against mine.

I was just getting the full sensation out of her kiss when
suddenly I awoke.

Once again it was the illusion. I get it so often.

She warms my whole body whenever I get the illusion, filling
my thoughts more often than I can control.

As much as I want our lives to be united, it just will not work
out. She has got her life to live, and I have got mine to live.

But to live on her illusion is food enough to sustain me.

She has and possesses my heart, with the ability to replenish any
man with her love.

The Salt-Filled Sea
1971

I swim on and on relentlessly
Hoping to find the salt-filled sea.

Find it not it seems to be
When I look far and wide for the salt-filled sea.

I swim from pond to pond and brook to brook
Then down the valley I overlooked.

On I swim forever and ever
Find the sea it does seem never.

My travels take me far and wide
Never knowing if I'll reach the tide.

Now into a river and upon a dam
It seems forever that I have swam.

I am tired, but it is now too late
For I did not realize the river was so great.

On and on it seems to be
Just to find the salt-filled sea.

I don't worry, fret, or cry
I now wish I would quietly die.

The Wiser Man
1971

Lying before me are days that glisten
Like nothing before has ever shown.
So, my fellow people, please listen
To that which a wiser man has to say
And that which he has known.

The wiser man knows a lot
More than one often suspects.
So pay attention while time is still sought
Before this same thought this person rejects.

Pay attention while you still can and dare
Because before long, time fades away.
Leaving you alone in darkness and easy to scare
Like the never-changing masquerades.

That wiser man is sought by many people
And few find him very soon.
Like the present tower and steeple
That sit in the night as the ever-present moon.

You

1972

You are the sun during the day
You are the moon shining at night.
You are the stars smiling in the sky
You glow with every light.

You have got the sweetness as honey from a bee
You are as fragile as a pretty rose stem.
You are as fresh as the morning sea
You are as precious as the rarest gem.

You have got the beauty to hold my eye
You have got the love to hold my heart.
You are the ease within a sigh
You are the happiness in my heart.

You are my heart's desire
Though long I have been awaiting.
I'll never put out my fire
For you I have been contemplating.

Although you are young
You have got time on your side.
At times the bells have rung
As I've searched far and wide.

It seems a long time
That I have waited.
And then I find
For you I have contemplated.

It seems I am ill with love
For all I want to do is cry.

If it were not for the glittering stars above
I would just lie down and quietly die.

Yes, you are my dream come true
If only given a chance, we could find
That love is not all blue
You see, I would never let you out of my mind.

A Rock of Sorrow
1972

Often I am picked up
And thrown great distances.
When I land
You know I am
A rock of sorrow.

When I ricochet off something
To hit the ground
You know that I am
A rock of sorrow
Only to be found.

If I crash through a window
To land in a corner
You know that
I am
A rock of sorrow.

Then I'm picked up
And thrown at a bird
I yell, "Look out!"
Only then I'm not
A rock of sorrow
Only to shout.

A Tear
1972

A tear falls from my eye as I recall your precious touch upon my coarse but sentimental body. You were the sun shining during the day, you were the moon shining at night. You made me love you in every way, you glowed with every light.

Whenever your deep, radiant eyes chanced to glance at me, I wanted to melt, but I had to walk and act like I never saw you. I had to walk with honor, prestige, and dignity. You don't realize how many times I wanted to take you into my arms and press my warm and fragile lips upon yours in a deep showing and expression of my love for you.

A tear is forming in my eye right now, as I listen to the song "Love Me Tender,". It hurts so very much, because you did love me tender, and you did love me sweet!

Your last kiss was a memorable kiss. It crosses my mind so very often, as you do whenever I am lonely.

I will always love and remember you. Your radiant eyes, your soft, gentle hair, your caressing touch, your beautiful, fine body, and the person within it.

A tear I shed for you, my dear, and one leads to another and another because you will never know how much I loved you.

Easy to See
1972

When you smile at me
Or chance a look at me
You know that I am
Easy to see.

When I find April Love
Or watch birds of May
You must think that I am
Always this way.

When you think of me
Or when I think of you
You know that I am
Easy to know.

To see a cloud float by
With a tear in my eye
You know that I am
Easy to cry.

When I look into your precious eyes
Or when I watch you sway along
You know that I am
Ready to sing a song.

When I think of you
And you think of me
I have to be
Easy to see.

Whatever way
It seems to me

You know I will always be
Easy to you and me.

On it goes
Playing a game
It always shows
But never the same.

Easy to you
Easy to me
I will always be
Easy to see.

Home
1972

A home is not a home without love
Love is defined as being God.

This home possesses much love
God is in this home.

Often a home creates love
Love makes this house home.

Life to Live and Later Die
1972

A tree stands upon a hill
A bird calls to its mate.
A baby whippoorwill
Oh, but it's getting late.

Brooks run fresh and clear
Pinecones drop to the ground.
A babe is filled with fear
Stars never to make a sound.

The sun setting in the West
Light fades to dark.
The moon looks its best
The sounds of a lark.

Elk graze in a meadow
Fish jump in a lake,
Mountaintops covered with snow
Hills roll with the earthquake.

Life to live and later die
Gold a very precious metal.
Little girls to always cry
The wind blows each little petal.

Insects fill the air
A snake crawls in the grass.
Happiness is going to a fair
The water is clear as glass.

Love, a great desire
A bird sits unaware.
A tree is engulfed by fire
The bright moon's glare.

Stars seem always to shine
Cattle to always graze.
A heart the shape of a valentine
The words of poetry in a phrase.

Life to live and later die
A colonel in a brigade.
The months of June and July
A necklace made from jade.

A student at Yale
A child without a name.
The sound of a nightingale
A horse that is lame.

A deer jumps a fence
Elephants that have big ears.
Birds that show their excellence
Eyes filled with tears.

Life to live and later die
Lovers under the moonlight.
The beauty of a butterfly
A kiss in the twilight.

The sight of the morning mist
Life to live and later die.
The beauty of amethyst
Little boys to always lie.

To grow very old
As time quickly evades.
The wintery water is very cold
On the beautiful mermaids.

The fog is very dense
Rains fall from the sky.
This is the consequence
Of life to live and later die.

Loneliness
1972

My shadow usually follows me everywhere I go. Sometimes he
hides from me, but he is usually there, waiting to hear what I
have to say. Whenever I am lonely or just need someone to talk
to, he is there. He doesn't talk back, but he helps me make the
right decisions whenever I am in question about what to do.

In time of need, when no one else is around, I always have
my shadow to talk with. I can always extend my hand, and my
shadow always grasps it like I was the only friend he had.

We can be walking along with my head high, walking with
pride, and my shadow does also, because he knows I am there
to protect him and guard him against the night. My shadow
always hides at night and only comes out during the day when
he knows it is safe and he can see.

Never to Know Concealment
1972

Your eyes are like two stars in the distant heavens, shining with
the ultra-brilliance, never to know concealment.

Your hair is as a waterfall cascading down from an embankment,
flowing ever so gently, never to know concealment or
confinement.

Your face is like the prettiest rose in a garden full of the most
exquisite roses ever grown.

Your lips are like two perfect crystals sitting side by side.

Your touch is like the gentlest rain falling from a sky of gray,
never to know concealment.

Your heart is like the wind that blows each little flower, never
to know concealment, but loving everything and everyone it
touches.

Your eyes, your hair, your face, your touch, and your heart will
always live in my mind because these qualities are never to
know concealment.

Not a Place
1972

A cloud gently floating by, the sun sending its heat waves and ultraviolet rays to a planet that seems to be without a heart, a place that is not a place.

A place where deep feelings and sympathy are seldom found. A cold place, with cold bodies, cold minds, and cold hearts. A place that cares not for you, what you do or what you are.

A place where love is seldom found. A place where death is common. A place that has a name but is not a place.

A place where there are rolling hills, flowing waters, jagged mountains, gigantic oceans, and nothing. A place that is not a place!

Spinning Top
1972

A cloud floats by
A drop of rain falls to the ground.
All happens in the sky
Like a spinning top going 'round.

Love is like a spinning top
It hurts so very much.
Never knowing when to stop
Or who it is going to touch.

You speak of love
I want to cry.
It makes me wish
That I would die.

Another cloud floats by
Another drop falls to the ground.
All happens in the sky
Like a spinning top going 'round.

Love is an endless game
Although it happens every day.
It is never felt the same
In each little way.

Clouds float by
Love fills every heart.
Love floats by
Spinning tops are why.

The Rounding Stair

1972

A star shining so bright
The full moon's glare.
The fading day's light
Up the rounding stair.

A poet sings his song
A drop of rain falls to the ground.
Children know between right and wrong
Like a clock going 'round.

Up the rounding stair
Are birds in the sky?
Knowing what is not fair
Makes little boys ask, "Why?"

A sound of joy
Dust filling the air.
A girl playing so coy
Like a rounding stair.

The day's last light
Filling the air.
The moon shining so bright
Up the rounding stair.

All ends with a glance
Toward the ending fair.
Eyes filled with romance
For the rounding stair.

The Same Old Story
1972

Everywhere I go
Everything I do
It's the same old story
Through and through.

It matters not
What I hear about you
It's the same old story
Either old or new.

I can't go far enough away
Without hearing
The same old story
Throughout the day.

Morning and night
All through the day
It's the same old story
In every way.

I travel far
I travel wide
Always searching
For the tide.

Everywhere I go
Everything I do
It's the same old story
Through and through.

The Sounds That Shadows Make
1972

A flick of the candlelight
Shining through the window.
All takes place on a winter night
Slowly it's beginning to snow.

The sounds that shadows make
Unsure sights that plague the mind.
Your breath it seems to take
Your heart slowly begins to wind.

You startle at every sound
Your heart the pounding of a drum.
Eyes searching all around
For the things not to be found.

The flick of the candlelight
Shining through the door.
Under the moonlight
In an old, rundown store.

The sounds that shadows make
Eyes searching all around.
Silence will soon break
If things are not to be found.

The sounds that shadows make
Unsure sights that plague the mind.
All happens in the night
In an old, rundown store.

The Wind Is Most Beautiful
1972

Grain fields wave gently in the summer's warm, gentle wind as
it softly prevails from a southwesterly direction.

A distant bird of prey soars high in the constant current of
endless wind, searching for its late-afternoon meal.

Wild roses sway from side to side as if they were never made for
stationary purposes.

Our country's flag stands projected out from the pole on which
it sits as the pole gently sways back and forth in a relentless,
rhythmic motion, keeping the beat of a pendulum.

But the wind is most beautiful! It has the ability to gently caress
the ocean waves and yet at the same time tear a tree from where
it stands. The wind is most beautiful.

It transports clouds of tomorrow in its upper limits while
spreading pollen from the most precious flowers to pollinate
others.

The winds blow the ocean spray against the mighty monoliths
that guard the sea.

The wind is most beautiful to only those who perceive it as so.

A Song of Love

1973

A song of softness, a song of love echoing in the background.
The moon rising in the blue-tinted heavens, the soft gentle
wind caressing a face of sorrow, a heart of disbelief in life. But I
trust in God to lead me in the right direction. Only He can help
me make the right decisions.

Often I take long walks, seeking peace of mind, solitude, and
stability. Something or someone to help me hold my chin high
and walk with courage and assurance, without fear, like a song
of love.

A tree ravaged by fire tells the story of my heart. It has been
burned so many times, yet after the flames have subsided, it
seeks new life. A life to grow straight and very free, free from
harm.

With each new love I chose, I left a part of me deeply embedded
within their shadow as they disappeared into the black, sullen
night. Like a song of sadness, like a song of sorrow, like a song
of love.

Admiration
1973

The tide rolls in with the gentleness of a sunray bearing down
upon each object within its grasp.

The wind picks the spray from the surf and carries it deep
inland to kiss the Earth with the dampness of a spring shower.

All of this takes place as I sit here among the flowers in solitude
with only myself and God to answer the questions I formulate
within my mind.

I guess I should be classified as a lone, proud, fire-scarred tree
in the middle of a wilderness. Standing so straight and rigid,
free from disease and the many other plagues that fill the Earth.
Standing alone and yet so very free, free from most harm that
might befall me.

My strength is all that supports my scarred-up frame. Standing
as a king among his followers. The majestic beauty of those
below and surrounding me. Such peace and tranquility are
within the eyes of all those who look to me for guidance and
support they find not within themselves.

I am the loudness in their whispers, I am the peace in their
violences, and I am the strength within all their weaknesses as
they look with admiration toward me.

Come Swing with Me
1973

Come swing with me
We will swing together
We will swing so free
You and I together.

Come swing with me
And reach for the sky
We will float together
As if to fly.

First I push you
This way then that
Then you push me
Up and down
Forth and back.

Come swing with me
We'll swing all day
Just wait and see
There is a way.

Let me swing with you
We'll swing together
Can't you see?
We were meant for the other.

We will swing all day
And nighttime too
Come swing with me
So we'll have something to do!

The Pounding of a Heart
1973

The pounding of a heart
Rolling hills across the land
Beauty that stands apart
Oceans that are so grand.

Tastes that are sharp
Sightings of an unknown fellow
The sounds of a harp
Throughout a meadow.

A massive tree left unmarred
By a raging fire
A stroll down the boulevard
Is a known desire.

Reflections of a lost lake
In a song of harmony
Love brings heartache
For you and for me.

A song and dance
Under the night light
Leads to romance
For those who are right.

The pounding of a heart
Like a big brass drum
Sorrow has its part
In a world of stardom.

The happiness of a clown
In the summer evening
On the far side of town
It's a real happening.

The pounding of a heart
Deep inside a brain
Time has its part
Like a stained-glass windowpane.

Steam reaches up toward the sky
True friends are always apart
Some people seem to never die
With the pounding of a heart.

A Lonely Heart
1974

I travel around here and there
Looking for a place to rest my head.
I long not to have a care
To take with me when I go to bed.

What a lonely heart
She says I possess.
She doesn't know she tears me apart
When she leaves me in distress.

It seems I sit here all alone
Everything plaguing my mind.
With no one to call my very own
Tells me I left something behind.

What a lonely heart
I shall always have.
It seems love will never start
For a lonely heart like mine.

I will make someone happy
Someday it will be.
Just wait and see
Even if I am a lonely simile.

To have a lonely heart
Like water down a valley.
Never to have a start
Having a lonely heart.

Be
1974

As soon as a man is emitted from his mother's womb, he runs
to his master and waits for his instructions. A good man listens
to his master and carries them out with proficiency.

He should be one who everyone wishes to be like, one who
is looked upon with admiration and predominant to everyone
without being overbearing.

He should be prominent in the things he does and not do them
as to complicate others.

Be cautious and be wise, and upon you will rest everyone's eyes.

Live a great life so you can die great!

Brown-Eyed Girl
1974

Everywhere I go
I think of her love,
She's the brown-eyed girl for me
That I think so much of.

To live without her
Is such a crime.
Dreaming of her often
Takes all my time.

That brown-eyed girl
She's for me.
My heart's in a whirl
Though it seems not to be.

She wanted to marry
Along the way,
The burden of love I'll carry
Whichever is the way.

I love her dearly
That is for sure.
I wouldn't mistreat her
For that is the Golden Rule.

I Loved You
1974

I loved you for the things you did and said to me.

Now I love you for everything you say and do because I know I can't have you.

I loved you because you were young in both mind and heart.

I loved you because you were you in every unknown part.

I loved you because you were the difference between night and day.

I loved you for every glance you happened my way.

I love you on this day.

And tomorrow too.

In every way.

If I Could Make a Wish

1974

If I could make a wish, I think I would wish for her to love me.
I would wish for her to hold me, and touch me, and love me
with her eyes, and especially her heart.

If I could make a wish, I would wish for, well, let's just say her!

If I could make a wish, let's just say, "I would make a wish."

Life
1974

All individuals are assigned their place in life
in accordance with the sacred order of fixed obligations and
circumstances, and that each individual has at least the right or
satisfaction of knowing his precise place in the universal order
of life according to basic law.

The computative minds of certain individuals are so unusual
as to perplex the natural emphasis placed on the order of life.
When in many cases, the related aspects of life and its many
faces are so great that they disrupt life in its quantity.

Life will always be so until there is no more spring, summer,
fall, or winter.

As the Bible states:

Lean not unto our own understanding!

She, Would

1974

Her soft brunette hair cascading down to her fragile shoulders
from her small, unique head. Her hazel-brown eyes searching
the area for that which I wish she would find in me.

Her tiny, delicate hips swaying from side to side as she gently
meanders with the minute, rhythmic motion of that of a
pendulum. Her precious, dainty hands reaching out to touch
that which is not there. Her warm and sympathetic heart crying
out for love, without her grasping it.

All this she holds, plus untold quantities that are indescribable.

She is very special and would mean something to any man who
could call her his own.

She, would be her name!

The Words

1974

The words are few
And so far apart
I think of her,
And it breaks my heart.

I think of her often
And cannot bear
A pillow is to soften
Not to tear.

The words to her
Are like poetry to me
She makes me blue
When I make my plea.

I cry to her over
And over again.
The love for her
Will always remain.

The words to the song
Are soft and broken
To be so wrong
Yet not to be spoken.

The words are from me
Whatever the way
You'll have to agree
There's nothing more to say.

Try to See It My Way

1974

If you try to see it my way
We will work things out.

Not necessarily today,
But it will be brought about.

The things that lovers say
Sometimes breaks my heart.

When I cannot find the way,
It's so hard to start.

Try to see it my way
For once in your life.

Leave it to me,
And you'll be my wife.

You in My Prayer

1974

Each evening as I fall to sleep
To lie in my bed
Always wondering
If we were to be wed.

Many times throughout the day
Depressed by life's care.
Always remembering
You in my prayer.

When daylight has gone
I sit in my chair.
Always remembering
You in my prayer.

Now you know, dear,
How much I really care.
Again to remember
You in my prayer.

An Old Man in America

1975

An old man sits next to a dog
With a care unknown to all.
He leans upon a worn-down log
Upon which he's placed his shawl.
Hello, America
Do we know this man?

He wonders how lonely
Can this troubled life be?
Knowing he's not the only
To share his drudgery.
This man sounds familiar
Doesn't he, America?

The old man meanders by an orphan home
And feels the same tie.
He wishes that he were not alone
and prays that he might die.
America
We know this old man!

A little girl looks out a window
Pleading with crying eyes.
The old man knows he's found a friend to know
And wonders why he cries.
Yes, America
It is him!

The old man visits the girl each day
Although he has no home.
He grows to love her more each way
She wonders why he's so alone.

Did America do this to you
Old man?

Then one day the old man doesn't come
She's so afraid he will never appear.
Weeping is only the minimum
Her eyes are crying and filled with fear.
This happens often in America
Goodbye, old man.

No one knew the old man had died
Except the heartbroken little one.
Now she has no one by her side
Escape from loneliness will never come.
A part of America dies
With men like you, old man.

She feels within her heart
The old man's absence in every way.
They should not be apart
God love him, she would always pray.
This old man and little girl
Are you and I, America.

The ties between them were so very close
Looking through that windowpane.
Now she only stares at the signpost
Of the orphan home, her domain.
Goodbye, America
We love you.

Our Prayer
1975

Dear God, we pray
In our Father's name,
You have guided us straight
And left us no shame.

Trying to live
According to your will
Makes us strive
To mend all ill.

To bring you into our hearts
Was easy to do
If all we needed
Was faith in you.

Each day we live
Most cautiously
Knowing not life's truth
Or fantasy.

All these precious moments
Dear God, we pray,
Will be with us always
From day to day.

Golden

1976

I have to believe
That we were golden
I have to believe
That it is true.

Whenever skies
Of darkness were upon us
We never let them
Stand in our way.

Whenever things
Would confront us
We would work them out
In every way.

I have to believe
That it was right.
I have to believe
In belief itself.

Whichever way
We seemed to turn
That way
Was the best way.

I have to believe
In only what I know.
I have to believe
In belief itself.

We struggled and toiled
Along the way.
Making the most
Of each new day.

This went on
for months and months
Believing the bond
Was ever so strong.

Unknown to me
She was not in love.
Making me turn
To the Almighty above.

I have wept
And I have prayed.
A lot of both
For each day.

In my
Hour of darkness
The hurt
Would not subside.

I walked
In the Valley of the Shadow
Searching for that someone
To call mine.

I have to believe
In what I believe
And what I believe
Is that we were golden.

Should I Help or Run?
1976

The streets are wary and dark
No place for a babe like me.
Wandering from place to place
So much is there to see.

A cry in the dark
Breaks stillness all around.
Wondering where it came from
Makes me ponder and stare.

A little girl cries
With a frantic voice.
Makes me hesitate
But leaves me no choice.

From what direction did it come?
I know not where.
Should I help or run?
I do not dare!

The night's silence
Is broken again.
By the shrill voice
Of a girl in pain.

Should I help or run?
I do not dare.
The sounds are so vivid
In the brisk autumn air.

What is she doing alone?
She should be with her mother.

Should I help?
Or should I take the other?

The break of dawn
Shines bright as the sun.
The hesitation is broken
I should not run.

No More

1977

Sitting here
Without you tonight
Leaves my heart so uptight
I can't go on no more.

Without your love I could die
Without your love I will cry.
I can't go on another day
I just can't go on no more.

Holding you not
Within my arms
I can't go on another day
I just can't go on no more.

When I see you leave my door
I can't bear the pain no more.
I can't go on no way
I can't go on another day.

If you were here tonight
Everything would be all right
I would be so uptight
Things would be out of sight.

As I dream of you tonight
Things will be so right.
Thinking of you in every way
Will get me through another day.

Won't You Love Me?
1977

Please say you'll love me
I don't think I'm really that bad.
I know that you are lonely
I know that you are sad.

If you'll reach out and touch me
You'll find I'm not sad
To love is good and healthy
It will make your sad heart glad.

Loving me would bring you joy
The world has much in store
There's so much we could try
By opening the door.

A field of yellow daisies
By the proud, majestic peaks
Are always in their glory
For you and I to seek.

So with my hand within your hand
And our love to keep us warm
Let's start a journey with no end
Another love is born.

Thinking of You
1978

Here in a quandary
Life goes on.
Thinking of you
With each new dawn.

Often I sit alone
No one around.
Thinking of you,
Not making a sound.

Thoughts running wild
So vivid on my mind.
Only happiness
Could you and I find.

Thoughts I express
Straight from my heart.
You are always there
Never to part.

Thinking of you
All of the time
Leaves my feelings
In a constant bind.

Knowing not
which way to turn
I guess for me
I'll never learn.

Deeply I submit
My feelings for you.
Thinking of you
Is all I can do.

Touch You Again

1978

When will I touch you again?
As each day slips by
With agonizing pain
Never knowing the reasons why.

"When will I touch you again?" I ask
It seems not today or tomorrow.
Ahead of me lies an unbearable task
And my heart's filled with much sorrow.

The reasons why, I do not know
All I can do is live for today.
Letting my life grow
Instead of crying it away.

Often do I cry
Throughout the night and day.
Deep inside my heart
Going all the way.

An endless stream
Down my cheek.
An unfulfilled dream
Ever so meek.

To touch you again
Seems not so real.
I am filled with much pain,
But I still feel.

Wandering
1978

Within the realms of my nomadic wandering, from obstacle
to obstacle, lies my search for the reasons why, for the reasons
themselves.

Constantly meandering, wandering like a stranger in the dark,
searching for that light that never or will not ever be found.

It seems like an untouchable dream on the verge of becoming
the touchable in the most incandescent way.

An eclipse of the unknowing upon the knowing, of obstacle
upon obstacle, and of the unreal sitting upon the real.

Constantly wandering from here to there, only to leave there
and end up who knows where?

A journey that will never cease to keep me from wandering
within the realms of my mind.

A New Life to Begin

1979

As we grow old
We shed an old skin
With each day
A new life to begin.

We sometimes get bored
With the life we live.
But onward we go
A new life to begin.

We search over again
For peace to be found.
At times so lost
Upon breaking new ground.

Never pleased
With what he have.
Always looking
For a new life to begin.

Along the Way
1979

Here it is
the middle of the day
A little-known path
I walk along the way.

It is so hard
To take the first step.
But it's the beginning
For a future to get.

I have struggled and toiled
Along the way.
But now I'm excited
For my first day.

I have waited
So very long
For my chance
To come along.

Living my life
From day to day.
To accept my journey
Along the way.

I Find
1979

Within the shadows of my mind
I find I am at peace.
With a world of generosity
A world of hidden love
A world of hidden kindness.
My peace stretches out
To every nook and cranny.
To all that seems untouchable
It stretches as the sea
That fills every shoreline
At the highest of high tides.
And it stretches to fill every wall
Of an embossed cavity
Filled to its capacity.
I find the peace within my heart
Is so very real
So very whole
What I find
Is what I find
Within my mind.

The Future
1979

Walking a crooked trail
Step after step.
I go unafraid
Of what lies in wait.

Onward I go
Looking to see
What my future will hold
Within my tranquility.

I see not tomorrow
What is held for me
I live each day
For what it is to be.

I reach for the gold
At the end of the rainbow
And hope to hold
The peace of the future.

The Garden Flowers
1979

Among the garden flowers,
Shimmering with beauty,
Are the spring showers
That make them so pretty.

They grow with fragrance
Throughout the day.
Noticed with each glance
Along the way.

A rose stands so tall
In the evening light.
So big yet so small
What a beautiful sight.

I see a tulip
So large and strong.
There it will sit
All the day long.

All the garden flowers
Begin to grow old.
Some leave tomorrow,
A story untold.

Withering with age
They all seem to be.
Life goes on
It is to be.

Me
1979

I am me,
Yes, I am!

I have many faults, but I am still me.
I have a warm personality, a warm smile,
and a fragrant sound when I say,
"Good day!"

It is great to be who I am,
Me!

To love the world,
and those within it,
is such a beautiful feeling.

To love each human being
As a separate entity.

To have a heart big enough for all to possess
Their own separate chamber of uniqueness.

To be who I am,
Me!

(Such a glorious feeling!)

My Mind
1979

As I sit here, I think, How lonely can this life be?

To be among friends and those who love me, yet so alone in the chasms of my mind.

Searching for the real, the nonexistent happiness that is seldom found within the cataclysms of thought.

Reaching and striving for the all and real, yet so unreal to my fingertips.

Like a most vivid dream or premonition that has not materialized. On the brink of discovery between fact and fantasy, illusion and reality.

My mind says I am strong, fearless, and willing; opportunity tells me I am expendable and subject to defeat.

My mind chooses my destiny of strength and willingness to succeed, leading me on a journey to the depths of reality.

Although opportunity tells me different, I look forward to the day when I can laugh and proudly look back and be thankful for letting my mind control me and my destiny, through Jesus, our Lord.

No Sight
1979

Walking a lonely trail
In the middle of the night
Is a child reading Braille?
He has no sight.

From letter to letter
From tree to tree
It will not get better
For him to see.

He lives
By smell and touch
To all he gives
So very much.

To each he loves
In every way.
He lets nothing
Prevent his day.

Although he has no sight
He's proud in every way.
He lives by night
From day to day.

Respect
1979

After so many years of following, worshiping, and praising these men I loved and admired, I soon find that I am now classified as one of those men.

Grown, matured, and developed as someone to be admired myself, looked upon with envy for what I am and who I represent.

It is a grand feeling to casually walk into a room full of people and be noticed by those who aren't usually observant of someone entering the room.

It is such a secure feeling to be looked upon with admiration and good spirit.

Respect is the secret! I guess respect is all that any man would want out of life, and to think that I have respect from others is such a glorious feeling that it is incomparable to most anything.

To be wealthy I am not, but to be respected is more wealth than all monies could purchase.

In order to be respected, one has to respect in return, and that is something I do best.

Searching
1979

I follow a path
Destination unknown.
I walk with courage
Afraid not.

Onward I go
Searching to find
The peace that is held
Within my mind.

Searching here
And there.
Searching almost
Everywhere.

Hard to find
It is to be
Eluding
My tranquility.

Walking in Loneliness
1979

On a frosted day of winter sunlight, I find myself walking alone.

Reaching but unable to touch. Striving but never to gain.

I know not why, but my heart is lonesome. I cry out for love,
while I am letting it slip away.

As I sit here shrouded by people, I feel the pains of solitude
bearing down upon me (as the wrath of the Almighty God
striking out against those who defy Him).

Although I have asked God for forgiveness for the wrongs I
have committed, they are all a sequential happening on the
journey to death.

Trying to be so very considerate is when I corner myself into
unrecognition. And then when I am taken into account, I am
slandered, tread upon, and ground into the dirt.

Often I am dwelled so deeply within my own thoughts that
I am startled into reality. I am contemplating the future and
forgetting the all-important present concept of existence.

Crying out for love while letting it slip away.

Do we not always crave what we already possess?

Walking
1979

As I walk, I hear the rain beating against the ground, thundering upon the leaves that rustle with the gentleness of a soft breeze.

I see the moon slowly take its place high in the heavens, casting a soft iridescence upon all that receives its rays.

But I walk on with nothing and no one to guide my footsteps.

I walk with the rhythmic motion of a pendulum beating to and fro. Each step taken coordinates with each beat of the swinging arm.

Onward, always progressing onward.

Looking proudly upon the past while gazing steadfastly into the future.

Projecting forward with optimism for a most beautiful life.

While looking back with confidence from the trials and errors I have experienced.

Walking with dignity of what I represent.

Within

1979

As I peer
Into your eyes
I see the depth
Of your soul.

I see the peace
Within your heart.
I see the wisdom
Within your mind.

I see the calm
That sits upon your breath.
I see the beauty
Within your breast.

I hear your softness
As you speak aloud.
I touch your presence
When you make a sound.

I see the warmth
Within your smile.
I feel the gentleness
Of your touch.

Within you,
I am.
I am
Within.

Changing
1980

Throughout history, one impression of man and his dominion over the Earth has remained constant—that man has a multitude of natures.

Finitely speaking, that conflict between good and evil, of higher nature and lower nature, the inner self and outer self, the attitudes of others and his own attitude. Always a conflict!

Consequently, how do we determine the real self if each feeling and experience is superseded by a different feeling and a different experience? Each taking precedence over the last. Never to be experienced in the same perspective as before.

One force pulling against the other.

Onward, progressively onward we go. Reaching for that ultimate goal we call "Happiness."

Reaching forth for a new dimension, striving for a new goal, a new drive, a new desire, and a new feeling.

Constantly, our dimensions, goals, drives, desires, and feelings are forever changing. One happening the beginning of the next, one experience the beginning of the next experience, and so on.

How can we differentiate the fantasy from the fact if this is the synopsis of life?

But for some of us, it comes easier to distinguish one from the other. That conflict between good and evil, of higher nature and lower nature, of inner self and outer self.

And what the heck of others' attitudes? Your attitude is what is important because according to God, you are the most important person in your life other than He.

The sooner we as human beings would realize this fact, the better off this world would be. Not only for you but also me.

One step preempting the next, one change preempting the next change, and so forth. Constantly moving on and changing throughout the process.

The one constant thing in life is change!

Condemned

1980

Throughout man's existence upon Earth, man has maintained superiority over his counterparts: the insects, the aquatics, the fowls, and the beasts.

Still, he is able to culminate the disaster of his own domain via pollution of every quality known natural to him.

It has been standard policy for man to venture through unknown paths and contaminate their very existence. What was pure and clean is now unfit, imperfect, and unsanctified.

Through man and his uncleanness, the Earth (our home as we know it) is hanging by its last strand to the reality of being what it is.

Homo sapiens, as we know him, has all but destroyed his own house in which he lives.

He has polluted the ground from which he cultivates his food, the water with which quenches his thirst, even the air that hypothetically permits him to exist another day.

I condemn you, MAN! But, then, I condemn myself, for I am "Man" also.

A Dream

1980

Last week I had the strangest dream I have ever had. I dreamed
that the world was filled with love and not filled with war.

I dreamed that the whole world was at peace, and things were at
ease and at rest. I dreamed that all was calm. I dreamed the most
rewarding dream I have ever dreamed before!

Never have I dreamed a dream like this dream, not ever.

This dream was really a dream to top any other.

If all would only dream a dream like this dream, maybe we
could put an end to war.

Feelings
1980

As I sit here searching the real person that sits upon my heart, I realize that sometimes existence is cruel and harsh. Only as it is conceived within each individual, though.

I find it a most challenging experience to start my life over again. So many disenchantments coupled with so many rewards.

So many mind-boggling happenings and yet such ecstasy to correspond with them.

Only to be accepted for what it is, a most rewarding experience! Another most enchanting experience among many to come.

As I sit here, the real person inside me tells me I am strong, stern within limits, and steady like a rock.

My past experiences have developed me into a much stronger person. Everything happens for the better! All circumnavigates around feelings, and feelings are the basis for existence.

Without feelings, we would be in a cold, lifeless void with cold, lifeless bodies circumferencing us.

The good Lord made us with feelings to weep over the misfortunes and laugh with the corresponding joy.

To weep and to laugh, I have done both. And I will probably do both many times to come.

I feel not sorry for the many times I will weep, but they are both part of life.

I look forward to the times I will laugh again. I do not look forward to the times I will weep, but they are both part of life.

With joy, there is sorrow, and conversely. Each plays a major role in the synopsis of life.

One is not without the other!

Life is for the living, let the dead bury the dead.

Influence
1980

Throughout the timespan of man's existence upon the Earth, a most dominant factor is the relative impact one entity has upon another entity. One thought channel taking precedence over another thought channel, one individual having a superior thesis over his rival.

Throughout existence, this fact has proven itself many times over.

Look at the superior influence that Marc Anthony had or even Hitler himself! Leading blind people into the blind.

One entity partaking the aspects of a supreme being entirely. Acting and carrying the administrative role with unknown evolutions.

Being superior only to himself. Being a master of those who are meek and hesitative, leading those followers and himself to realms of obliqueness.

Being a mastermind of his objective: to build a kingdom of superiority, only to be destroyed by another, more powerful mastermind.

For each man must reap what he has sown.

Let not one man stand in the path of another who is moving forward.

My Companion
1980

As I sit upon the bank of a river slowly meandering down a valley, it is evident that no one but God could have arranged everything so perfect!

Each petal of a flower, each leaf of a tree, even the blades of grass, all serve their purpose in the never-ending revolving sequence of existence.

God created the sight, sound, and smell of the Earth for His companion, "Man," to enjoy.

What a magnificent feeling it gives me to know that whenever I am troubled or plagued with problems, I have my Maker, Master, and Lord to turn to for advice and guidance.

Whatever the confrontation, I always have my Lord God awaiting to strengthen me and fill me with His everlasting love.

In the times of dire need and weakness, it is such a glorious sensation to know that if I so choose, I do not have to walk alone. My companion is always there.

Reach Out
1980

Have you ever reached out and touched, hugged, or even kissed someone who was unfamiliar to you?

Not everyone is within themselves or secluded within their own worlds.

Most of us are as loving, sentimental, and warm, as are the select few who demonstrate these qualities. The only restriction holding them back is the hesitative insecurity they have.

Most of us are crying and longing for the attention that we are deprived of.

All of us are insecure in the concept of not always being wanted or needed.

And it seems once we obtain this facet of life, we become unsettled, unhappy, and unsure because we think there is something more to offer us elsewhere.

If we only had the foresight of the future, things would seem to be much more simplified.

If only more of us would learn to reach out and touch, or hug, or even kiss someone whom we know not!

Stand Tall
1980

Tread not lightly
The water is so deep.
Be not afraid
Of being meek.

Stand with
Dignity and pride.
Wherever you turn
There is nowhere to hide.

Accept the things
That happen to you.
It is not always right
But it's always true.

Live each day
To its limit.
Life goes on
That is eminent.

Tomorrow
1980

Progressively onward
Day after day
I live a whole life
Unafraid of tomorrow
And what lies in wait.
Tomorrow I will seek
That which will
Make me more whole
That which will
Make me more knowledgeable
That which will
Make me more filled.
Tomorrow I will seek
Tomorrow again.

What Was to What Is
1980

Life has the tendency of evolving from what was into what is.
Once again we view it as a conflict. That conflict of changing
our present mode of existence into that better mode of
existence. The fear of the unknown.

Having the fear of 1) venturing into a totally new realm of living
standards, 2) not doing something in the manner we learned
how to do it in, and 3) the fear of learning something new.

As I said, it is also viewed as a conflict. That conflict of whether
to or whether not to.

A most hesitative, quandary, mind-boggling situation to be in.

Very seldom viewed, viewed upon as the betterment of we
human beings and our living standards, or mode of living
standards.

If not viewed upon with an open, challenging mind, we would
never change from what was into what is.

Where would man be today if a few men were not imaginative,
adventurous, and stimulated by the conquest of new thought
patterns? Would he still be dwelling in some cave or in some
lost, forgotten tunnel?

Are you satisfied existing in a world of what was to what is?

For we are the rulers of our own destinies!

Why Things Happen to Us As They Do
1980

God Almighty knows us before we are born.

He not only knows us but the circumstances that comprise our lives as well.

He can control our lives if we will only lend Him one of our ears. Even if we do not listen to Him, He still permits us to delve headlong into our existence with one problem intertwined by another problem.

With difficulty after difficulty do we travel through life's pattern.

But there is justification behind our troubles.

Do we benefit from our troubles?

The answer is:

Yes.

Jesus gives us only enough pressure from problems that He knows we can cope with. And yet, on the other hand, He only gives us problems to bear in those areas in which we are weakest.

The reason is to make us stronger and more committed to our Lord Jesus!

But not all of us believe in our Lord. Yet even in the unbeliever's heart, the Bible states:

One day we will all recognize Jesus as our Lord.

Deep Within
1981

My lips upon your lips,
My breath smothering your breath.

My eyes deep within your eyes,
Your breast upon my breast.

My love deep within your love,
Your heart deep within mine.

My life mingled in your life,
Your life deep within my heart.

My strength is your weakness,
Your strength is deep within mine.

I Walk

1981

I walk a path
The Lord guides my way.

I seek the peace
Within each day.

I falter often
As I walk.

Wondering why
I cannot talk.

I want to be perfect
Yet knowing I'm not.

Reaching for Jesus
Is all I've got.

Why I'm not perfect
I can understand.

Only Jesus
Had a perfect hand.

At the end of the rainbow
I reach for the gold.

Leaving tomorrow
A story untold.

Walking Alone
1981

At times in our lives
We feel the load
Of walking along
The troubled road.

We all must reap
What we have sown
For if we don't
We won't have grown.

Joy and despair
Go hand in hand
Reaching forward
Across the land.

Walking alone
Is such solitude
Reaching out
Is what to do.

Love
1982

Lord, it's true.
You love me most
For without you
I would be lost.

Is there anything
I can do
Without your love?
No, not without you!

Part-Time
1982

I did not ask to be born, but since the Lord granted me the breath of life, I am going to make the most out of my existence and reach for the gusto that is offered in serving God.

We come into this world with nothing, and we leave with nothing. But if we draw nigh unto God, He will draw nigh unto us.

If ye love me and keep my commandments, I will love and manifest myself unto you, sayeth the Lord.

Seek ye first the Kingdom of God, and all things shall be given you.

Delight thyself also unto the Lord, and He will bring you the desires of your heart.

If we live according to Gods' righteousness, He will meet our needs and more.

It is not often we obtain what we reach for, of course, unless it is through Jesus Christ. Only He can and will meet our needs.

When Jesus said this two thousand years ago, it was for those who put their trust in Him, and it still holds true.

We are either walking with or against God. There can never be a part-time Christian.

You cannot sin throughout the week and ask God to forgive you your sins on Sunday.

God doesn't work on a part-time basis!

Temptation
1982

God loves you, and He loves me. All we have to do is realize it
or become aware of it.

Breaking loose of our own little self-pity parties (that most of
us live in) can be very difficult if we do not have Christ in our
hearts. Even when we do have Christ in our hearts, Satan hits
us at our weakest and most vulnerable areas to try to destroy the
love of Christ that we have and the love that He has for us!

We must stay firm in Christ's word to overcome our enemy,
Satan.

Each day, many times over, we are tempted to eat of the apple,
as Eve was, and whether we do or not is entirely up to us as we
journey and pass through this life, bombarded by temptation in
all the ways.

Thank You, Jesus

1982

Thank you, Jesus, for the beauty
We see within and from our eyes,
Thank you, Jesus, for the depth
Within the skies.

Thank you, Jesus, for the life
You have given us this day,
Thank you, Jesus,
For letting us pray.

Thank you, Jesus, for the calm
That sits upon our breaths,
Thank you, Jesus, for the beauty
We hold within our breasts.

Thank you, Jesus, for the peace
We hold within our chastity,
Thank you, Jesus,
For our tranquility.

Through you, Jesus,
We are able to care,
Through you, Jesus,
We are able to share.

Through you, Jesus,
We are able to live,
Through you, Jesus,
We are able to love.

Thank you, Jesus.

To Choose
1982

We all have, do, or will love sometime in our lives.

The importance or the value we place upon that which we love
determines the magnitude or sincerity of our love.

Love can ultimately be described as being Jesus Christ. Without
Christ, there can be no love within us.

We humans can and do display various degrees of letting
Christ's radiance show within and through us.

We all have a mission to carry out while here on Earth, that of
spreading God's word through the love of Christ.

All have sinned and fall short of the glory of God, but just
because we have sinned doesn't mean we are classified as
sinners and condemned to hell.

God knows we are only human, which we prove through sin.

Although in Gods' eyes, there was only one true sinner—that
being Adam. For Adam condemned all mankind to a life of sin.
Adam had a most decisive choice to make.

The "enemy" attacked Adam, creating confusion, doubt, and
loss of faith within his mind, and Adam submitted and was
deceived into believing Satan, consequently resulting in mans'
life of sin.

God gives us all a choice of whom to follow.

Have you made the right choice?

Jesus will never force anyone to love Him. The choice is yours! Man cannot serve God and mammon simultaneously; therefore, a choice must be made.

At any time throughout our lives, we can choose to submit our lives to Christ, and He will accept us with open arms and love overflowing.

Christ died for the sins of you and I—the least we could do is serve Him!

Seeking
April 9, 1983

Sometimes,
While seeking my true self,
I think:

"Is existence meant to be so compounded by problems?"

The only response I find comes from deep within my soul.

My soul says to trust and believe in Christ, Jesus, for the true strength to deliver us from all evils that confront our lives.

It does seem so hard to trust in another being to meet our total needs.

Yet once we realize that all our needs can be met through Christ, if we only let Him, it is harder not to trust in Him.

Christ says that we must all become as little children first. Just as babies are dependent upon their mothers for life, so as we adults should be dependent upon Christ for all our needs.

Romans 8:31

If God be for us, who can be against us?

The Glory of God through Salvation

February 22, 1984

To the glory of God
From we who praise you
We lift up our hearts
And will always adore you.

Letting your true light shine
To all ends of the Earth
Helps make our job
Seem all that it's worth.

Your grace is upon us
though we don't deserve it
We were born in sin
And try to live without it.

Your word
Is the rock of salvation
Believing in you
Is the reason for all creation.

In His Presence
May 19, 1984

In your presence, Lord
There will I be satisfied
Over and over again
Forevermore.

In your presence, Lord
Comfort and warmth surround me
Knowing you're there
Forevermore.

In your presence, Lord
Will I put my trust
And find my strength
Forevermore.

In your presence, Lord
There will I be found
Always and
Forevermore.

Each Day

October 13, 1993

The seasons run from dawn to dusk,
Each day of the year, and end they must.

From fall to winter, spring to summer,
Each day filled with awes and wonder.

The seasons sometimes short or long,
Each day the beginning of a wondrous song.

The seasons of each day,
Sound each tune.
From dusk to dawn,
From rising to setting moon.

A Dog

July 2019

Walking along
By a dog with no name,
Singing a song
It's somewhat the same.

I sing the song
As best as I can.
The dog looks up at me
I wonder why he ran.

I give a whistle
He stops in his tracks.
I definitely see
Affection he lacks.

We start to develop
A bond not broken.
We see how important
Words are unspoken.

Changes

July 2019

A quivering leaf
Sits next to a window.
It's hard to believe
It is starting to snow.

The seasons change
With an almighty blast.
It seems only yesterday
I was mowing the grass.

It seems they change
Every six months of the year
And yet to arrange
The order so dear.

Change they must
It's the order of life.
Filled with trust
For the guiding lights.

To each new beginning
There is an end.
Love forever
Till it reaches the bend.

Elements
August 4, 2019

The sun shining bright
Through the windowpane
That lets in the light
Either stained or plain.

The clouds in the sky
Tell us rain is near
My eyes are crying
And filled with fear.

I've seen storms
Like this before
Tearing the land
And flooding the shore.

Never knowing
What to expect
The wind is blowing
As I suspect.

It blows dust
From the mountain
It blows mist
From the fountain.

The sky thunders and cracks
Afraid we will die
Our confidence lacks
From He in the sky.

Fantasy

July 31, 2019

Walking down a road
It seems without end,
Stories untold
Or never to begin.

It seems the end is near
Or never to start again,
I walk along in fear
Without a friend.

Reaching and searching
For that star well beyond
My unreachable self.

As distant as it is
It is mine,
However
I cannot touch it.

Never knowing the time
Or if I'll ever find
That peace of mind
All the time.

Reality is near
Fantasy is far,
Now I know
How alone we are.

I Hear, I See

August 4, 2019

I hear the whisper
Of the wind
As it gently kisses
The pines
With a brush of softness
To say goodnight.
I see the buck deer
Gently kneel down
Until it rests
Chin to earth
In the spot it so
Carefully prepared
For its massive body
To lie down upon.
He guards his herd
Of smaller bucks and does.
I see the birds of prey
As they settle into their perches
High in the dead old
Fire-ravaged pine tree
That sits without life
In a meadow so green
Filled with flowers
As colorful as the rainbow
That fills the dusk of sky.
As light fades to darkness
A gentle mist begins to fall.
As if God were to reach down
And caress each and all
With good blessings
For the night
To one and all.

Forever
July 2019

Looking for songs
In all the right places
Looking for hearts
That are so gracious.

Finding not
It forever seems.
I look far and wide
For my forever dreams.

I search far and wide
With no luck in sight.
Songs seem to hide
As I reach for the light.

To find that song
That fills my heart
I stroll along
With the morning light.

I cry over
And over again.
Never knowing
If or when.

Beginning to lose
That forever song
Helps me choose
All the day long.

Morning
August 2, 2019

Love sings
Like the morning dew
Upon the wings
Of a morning that's new.

I fly so high
With each gust of the wind
So high in the sky
Will the story begin.

Flying from gust to gust
Before the storm
Yield it must
Before the morn.

It takes refuge
In a big oak tree
After the deluge
All creeks run to the sea.

One would think
It would fill up
On the brink
Of the silver cup.

Knowing the difference
Between right and wrong,
This is the consequence
All the day long.

Tunes of affection
Fill the air
In the direction
Of a future stare.

She looks so fine
In the morning mist,
She'll be mine
After we've kissed.

Birds of a feather
Always flock together
This is a story
In all its glory.

Over and Over Again

August 1, 2019

I hear the whisper
of the wind
As it tantalizes my ear.
I hear the same old song
Over and over again
In my head.
I hear the rhythm
Of the drum
Constantly beating
Over and over again.
The tune in the background
Filling my head
With the same beat
Of a pendulum.
Back and forth
A constant motion
Never ending.
The kiss of the wind
Whispers into my ear again
Like the rhythm
Of the big bass drum.
Over and over again
A constant motion.
I taste the sweetness
Of love
In the air.

Tears of Life

July 30, 2019

The tears of life
Are common but true,
Never knowing
What to do.

Leaves you in
A constant haze,
Coming from within
The middle of a maze.

Never knowing,
What to do,
The tears of life
Are always true.

Always running
Down my face,
Leaving behind
Not a trace.

They fall
For no reason at all.
The reason I cry
I know not why.

The Bee

July 31, 2019

I hear the wind
Rustling through the brush,
A storm starts to burn
As the flowers begin to rush.

It happens often,
Time grows very short
For the bumble bee.

He flies from bush to bush,
From tree to tree,
Making his last stand.

From flower to flower,
He places pollen
To where they stand.

If he only knew the consequence of life,
How short his life would be
Flying from bush to bush
And tree to tree.

The Reason

August 1, 2019

Lying here
Thinking
Makes me wish
I were drinking.

A drink or two
Down the hatch
Even a Mountain Dew
To finish the catch.

Wishing I were
Running around
Instead, here I sit
Not making a sound.

Time passes by
We all grow older
I wonder why
We all get colder.

The passage of time
Brings a new season
Along the line
Time is the reason.

The Sun

July 2019

Raindrops fall
Rivers run.
All happens in the sky
Under the sun.

Life begins to grow
It seems to be
All happens below
The almighty sun.

As we look up
It is bright to our eyes
We fill our tea cup
With love from the skies.

A heart left unbroken
A dance that never ends
Words that are unspoken
Love that never bends.

The thought of a kiss
Under a streetlight
Even if it is not,
I search for the light.

The sun to always sit
High in the sky
A candle sits unlit
Wondering why.

Thoughts
August 1, 2019

Beginning to seek
That which is unknown
Those who are meek
Feelings are grown.

Thoughts are there
The meanings are known
Wondering where
The thoughts are grown.

Unsure and unaware
We look around
A cold-hearted stare,
Not making a sound.

I sit by a window
The light widens my eyes
I see life's show
Under the skies.

Time will only tell
A story untold
The ringing of a bell
Are times oh so bold.

Time tells a story
Not very old
In all its glory
Never untold.

Time

July 30, 2019

Time passes by
With the blink of an eye,
All happens together
No matter why.

The will to live
Is like no other,
No matter what we give
To be the other.

Time is like
The end of a song,
Bittersweet
To carry along.

All happens
Before the end
Of the song
All the day long.

Time has a way,
Of passing by,
Always wondering
Who may try.

To Remember
July 29, 2019

All the times
That I remember,
Always find
Special moments in September.

From youth to age
Time passes by,
From page to page
Like the sweetest lullaby.

I hear the sounds
That shadows make,
Life abounds
After the earthquake.

The hills roll
From side to side,
Each takes its toll
On the countryside.

Moments to remember
Are a special tune,
Always in October
Lies a hidden moon.

Singing

Walking along,
A river bed,
Singing a song,
Of which I'm fed.

The Spirit guides,
Those who listen,
Daylight subsides,
Letting the stars glisten.

I walk alone,
No one near,
I sing off tone,
Hoping no one can hear.

Led by the Spirit within,
He is so strong.
A new path I'll begin,
When I sing a new song.

Things to Remember to Forget

Forget each kindness that you do
As soon as you have done it.
Forget the praise that falls to you
The moment you have won it.

Forget the slander that you hear
Before you can repeat it.
Forget each slight, each spite, each sneer
Wherever you may meet it.

Remember every kindness done to you
Whatever its measure.
Remember praise by others won
And pass it on with pleasure.

Remember every promise made
And keep it to the letter.
Remember those who lend you aid
And be a grateful debtor.

Remember all the happiness
That comes your way in living.
Forget each worry and distress
Be hopeful and forgiving.

Remember good, remember truth
Remember heaven's above you.
And you will find through age and youth
That many hearts will love you.
A broken heart continues to tear me apart.

Unknown author

Be kind
Be loving
All this you'll find,
In being forgiving.

Now I continue my walk from "Life to Life."
Thank you for letting me share my journey with you.

CPSIA information can be obtained
at www.ICGtesting.com
Printed in the USA
BVHW081331090220
571821BV00001B/62